W9-AUF-678

EDITION

2010 TOP ROCK HITS
FOR GUITAR

Produced by
Alfred Music Publishing Co., Inc.
P.O. Box 10003
Van Nuys, CA 91410-0003
alfred.com

Printed in USA.

ISBN-10: 0-7390-7501-2
ISBN-13: 978-0-7390-7501-2

Crowd photo: © istockphoto.com / Milan Klusacek

ARTIST INDEX

CONTENTS

1, 2, 3, 4

Words and Music by
TOM HIGGENSON

One, two, one, two, three, four.

1. Give

ANOTHER WAY TO DIE

Words and Music by
DAVID DRAIMAN, DAN DONEGAN
and MIKE WENGREN

*All gtrs. tuned down 1 & 1/2 steps:

⑥ = C♯ ③ = E
⑤ = F♯ ② = G♯
④ = B   ① = C♯

Moderately ♩ = 108 (w/half-time feel)

*Recording sounds one and one half steps lower than written.

Verse 1:

14

Outro:

THE ANIMAL

Words and Music by
DAVID DRAIMAN, DAN DONEGAN
and MIKE WENGREN

*All gtrs. tuned down 1/2 step:
⑥ = E♭   ③ = G♭
⑤ = A♭   ② = B♭
④ = D♭   ① = E♭

*Recording sounds a half step lower than written.

Chorus:

22

The Animal - 10 - 5

Interlude:

Outro:

Nah, nah.

AWAKE AND ALIVE

All gtrs. in Drop D: ⑥ = D

Moderately ♩ = 84

Intro:

Words and Music by
JOHN COOPER and BRIAN HOWES

Chorus:

Chorus:

Elec. Gtr. 3 resume chorus fig. simile

wake, I'm a - live, now I___ know what I___ be - lieve in - side.

BURN IT TO THE GROUND

*All gtrs. in Drop D, down 1 1/2 steps:

⑥ = B   ③ = E
⑤ = F♯   ② = G♯
④ = B   ① = C♯

Lyrics by CHAD KROEGER
Music by NICKELBACK

Moderate shuffle ♩ = 124

Intro:

*Recording sounds one and one half steps lower than written.

**Elec. Gtr. 1 dbld.

1. Well, it's

P.M. - - - - - - - -

Verses 1 & 2:

mid - night,   damn right,   we're wound   up   too   tight.
(2.) scream - in' like   de - mons and swing - in' from   the ceil - ing.

Rhy. Fig. 1
Elec. Gtr. 1

Interlude:

Verse 3:

Tick-in' like a time bomb, drink-in' 'til the night's gone.

Well, get your

hands off of this glass, last call, my ass.

Well,

Chorus:

w/Rhy. Fig. 2 (Elec. Gtr. 1)

w/Rhy. Fig. 2 *(Elec. Gtr. 1) 1st 4 meas. only*

We're go-in' off to-night to kick out ev-'ry

(Ooh,_____ ooh._____) (Hey!)

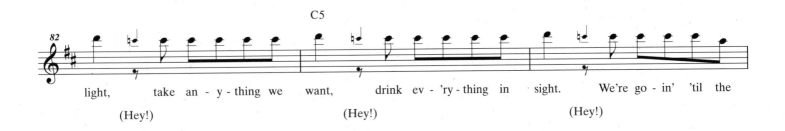

light, take an-y-thing we want, drink ev-'ry-thing in sight. We're go-in' 'til the

(Hey!) (Hey!) (Hey!)

world stops turn-ing while we burn it to the ground to-night.___

Elec. Gtr. 1

COUSINS

Lyrics by
EZRA KOENIG
Music by
CHRIS BAIO, ROSTAM BATMANGLIJ,
EZRA KOENIG and CHRISTOPHER TOMSON

Fast ♩ = 168

*Chords are implied.
Suggested strum pattern.

Verses 1 & 2:

1. You found a sweat-er on the o-cean floor.___ They're gon-na find it if you
2. Dad was a risk tak-er, his was a shoe mak-er. You, great-est hit two thou-sand

did-n't close the door.___ You and the smart ones sit out-side of their sight___ in a
six lit-tle list mak-er. Heard codes in the mel-o-dies, you heed-ed the call. Or you were

Cousins - 5 - 1

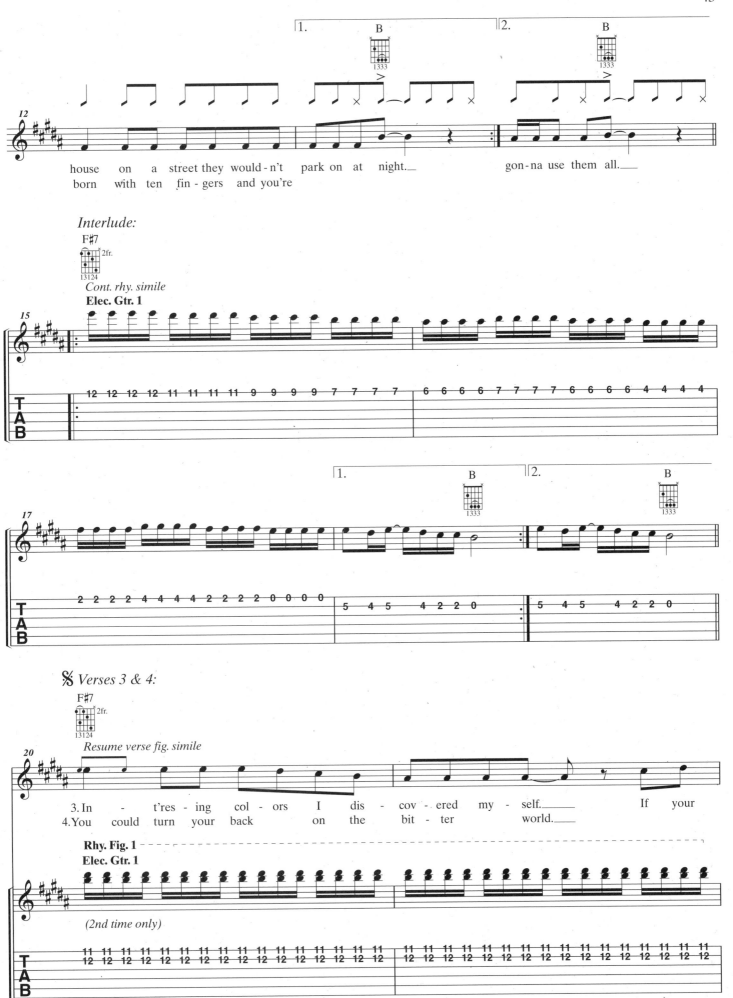

house on a street they would-n't park on at night.___ gon-na use them all.___

born with ten fin-gers and you're

Interlude:

F#7

Cont. rhy. simile

Elec. Gtr. 1

Verses 3 & 4:

F#7

Resume verse fig. simile

3. In - t'res - ing col - ors I dis - cov - ered my - self.___ If your

4. You could turn your back on the bit - ter world.___

Rhy. Fig. 1

Elec. Gtr. 1

(2nd time only)

46

HOLLYWOOD WHORE

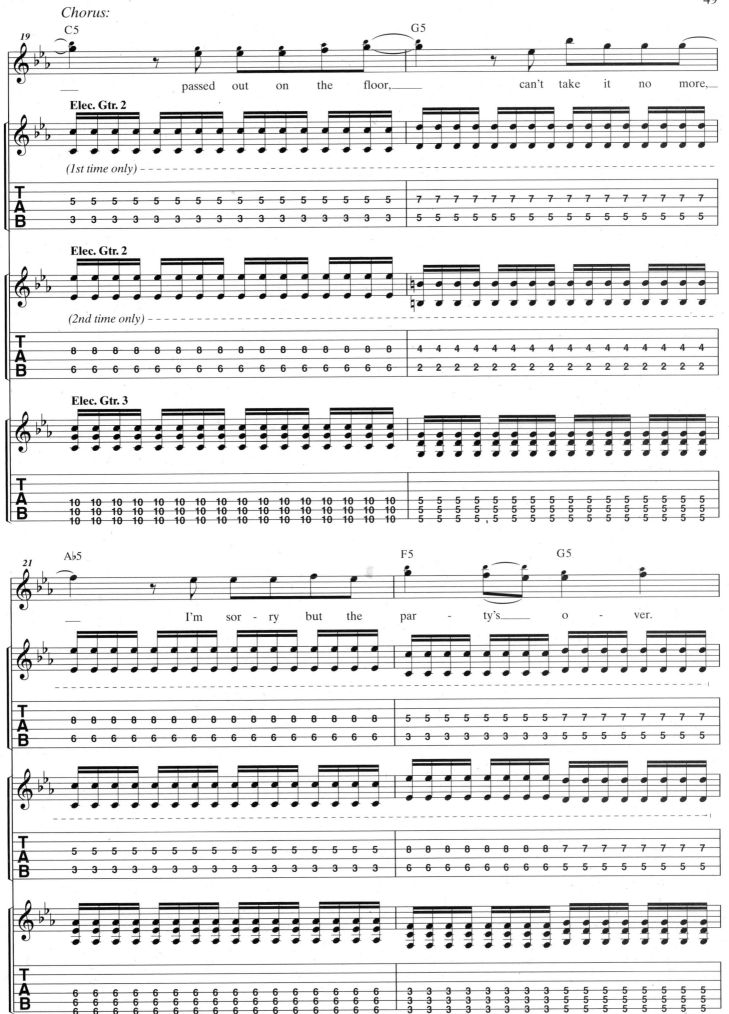

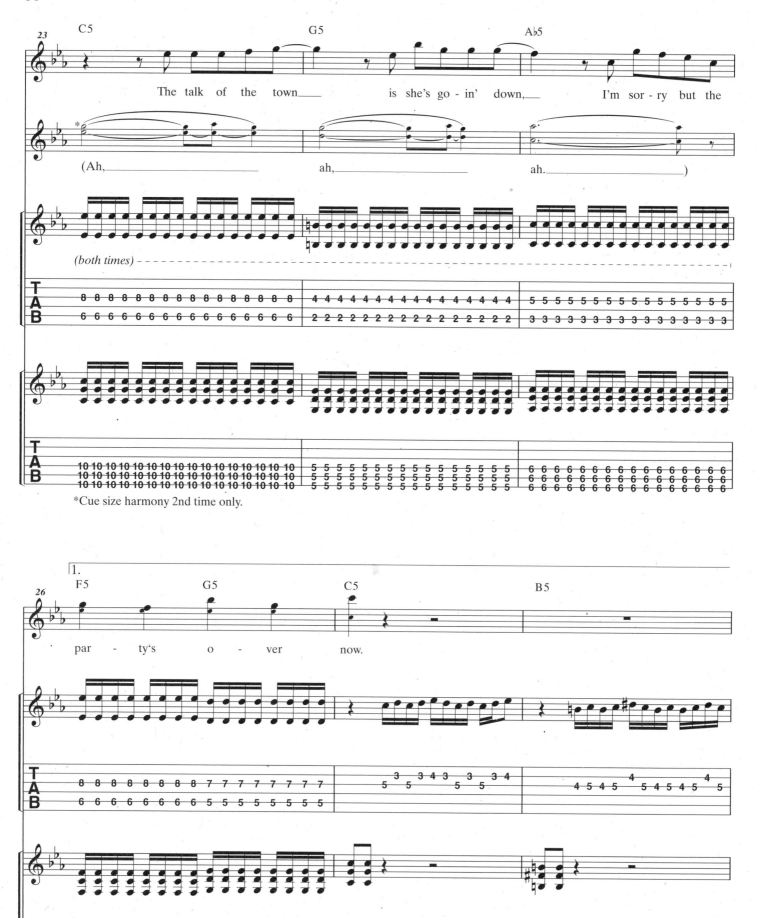

*Cue size harmony 2nd time only.

The talk of the town___ is she's go - in' down,___ I'm sor - ry but the

(Ah,_____ ah,_____ ah._____)

par - ty's o - ver now.

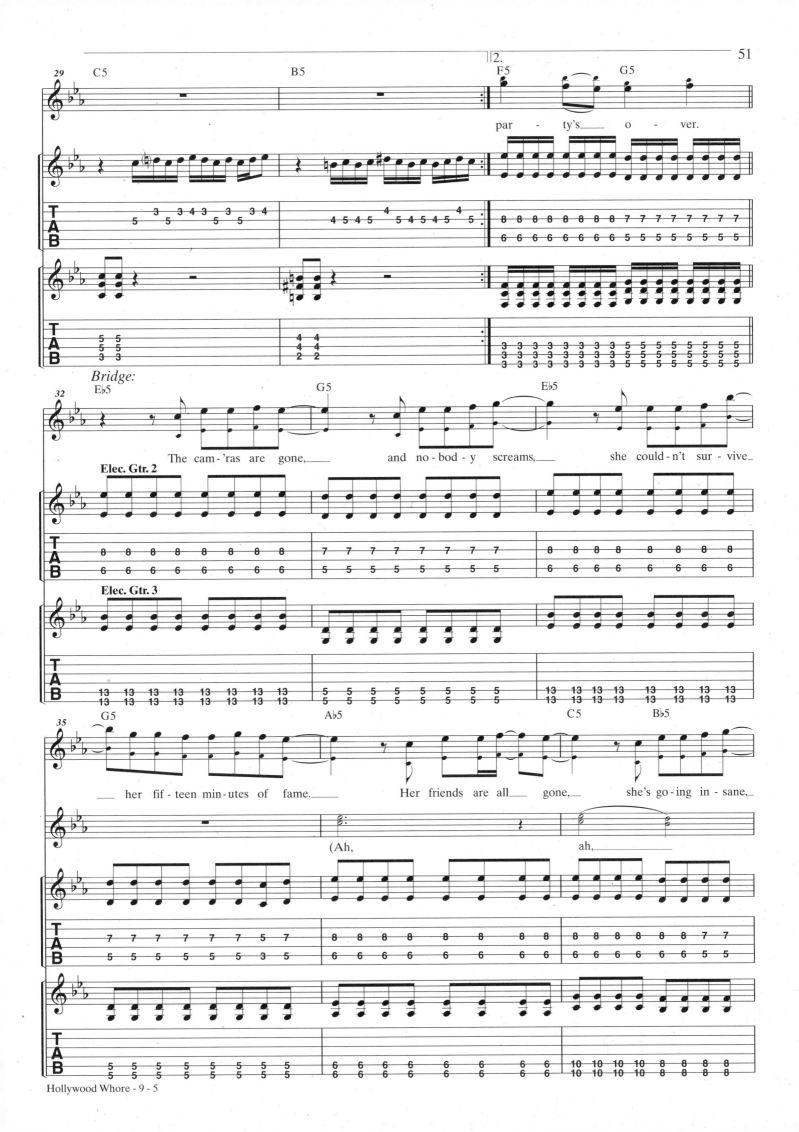

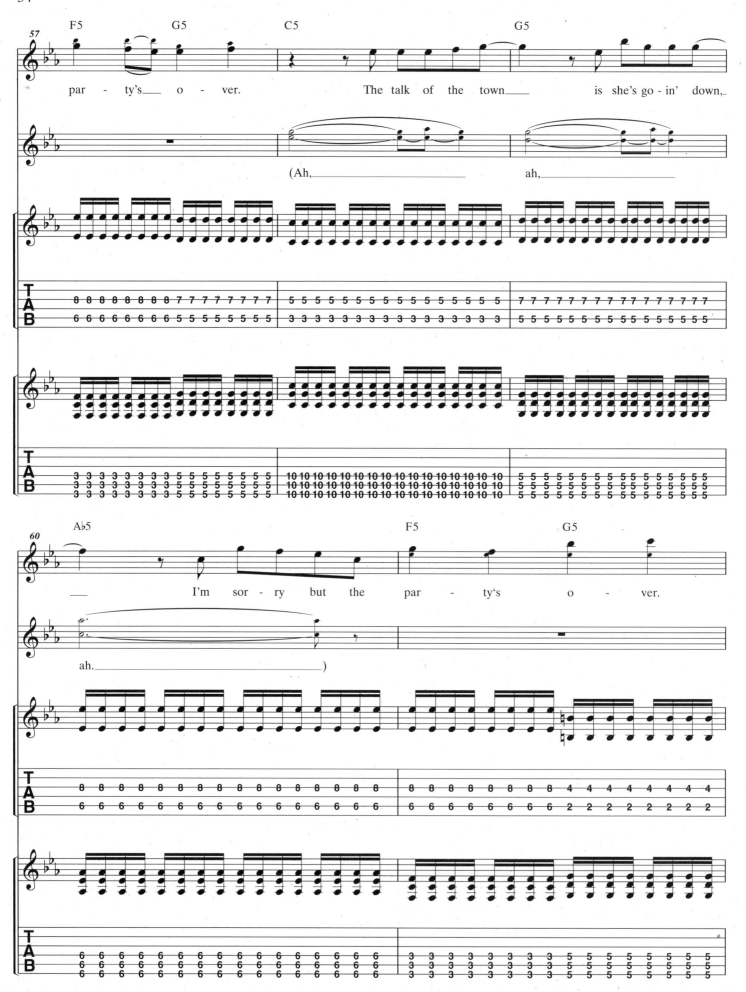

Outro:

Ha, ha, ha. Don't let the door hit ya where the good Lord split ya, honey. *Ha, ha, ha.*

EAST JESUS NOWHERE

Lyrics by BILLIE JOE
Music by GREEN DAY

Say a prayer for the family.
Drop a coin for humanity.
Ain't this uniform flattering?
I never asked you a goddamn thing.
(To Chorus:)

HATE MY LIFE

Lyrics by TYLER CONNOLLY and CHRISTINE CONNOLLY
Music by TYLER CONNOLLY, DAVID BRENNER
and DEAN BACK

*All Gtrs. tune down 1/2 step:

⑥ = E♭   ③ = G♭
⑤ = A♭   ② = B♭
④ = D♭   ① = E♭

Moderately ♩ = 112

Verse 1: (0:02)

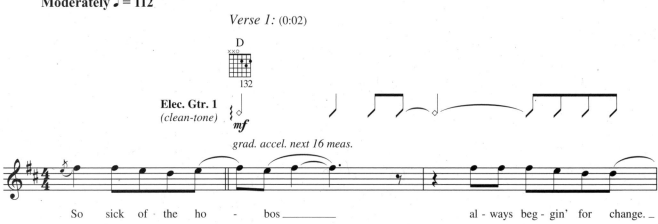

So sick of the ho - bos ___ al - ways beg - gin' for change. ___

*Recording sounds a half step lower than written.

___ I don't like how I got - ta work ___ and

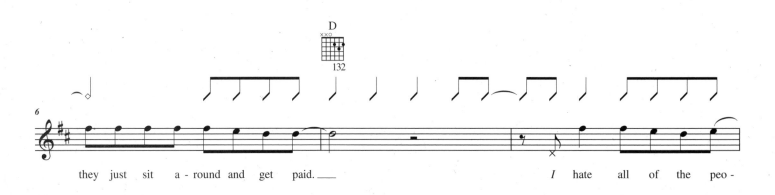

they just sit a - round and get paid. ___ *I* hate all of the peo -

Hate My Life - 8 - 1

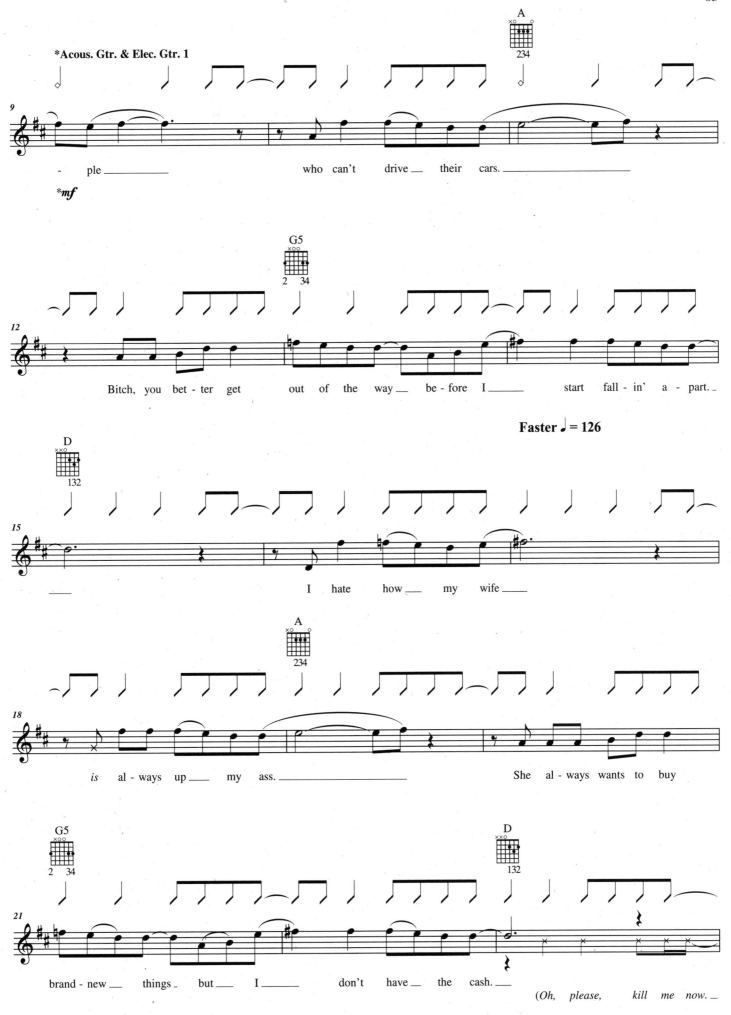

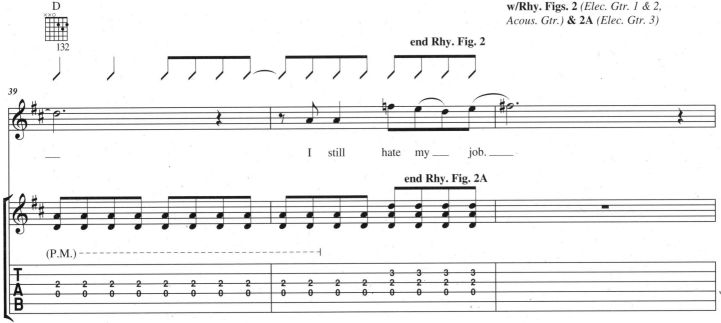

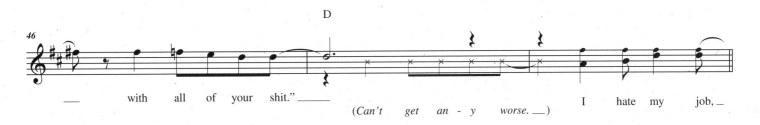

Hate My Life - 8 - 4

Chorus: (1:35)

w/Rhy. Fig. 3 *(Elec. Gtrs. 1-3, Acous. Gtr.)*

_____ all of my rich friends, _ I hate ev - 'ry - one _____ to the bit - ter end.

_____ Noth - in' turns out right, _____ there's no _____ end in sight. _

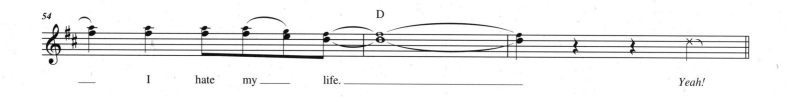

_____ I hate my _____ life. _____ *Yeah!*

Interlude: (1:50)

Elec.
Gtr. 4
(w/dist.)

w/Rhy. Fig. 2 *(Elec. Gtrs. 1-3, Acous. Gtr.)*

Hate My Life - 8 - 5

I hate that I can't ___ tell ___

Verse 3: (2:05)
w/Rhy. Fig. 2 *(Elec. Gtrs. 1-3,*
Acous. Gtr.) 2 times
w/Riff C *(Elec. Gtr. 5) 15 times*
w/Riff C1 *(Elec. Gtr. 4) 12 times*

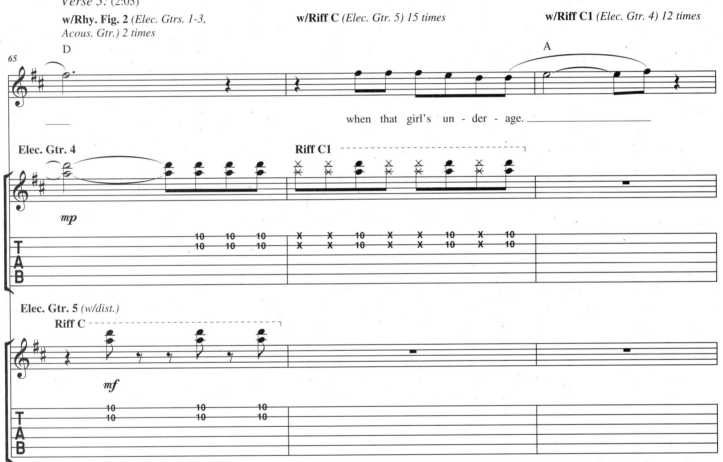

when that girl's un - der - age. ___

Elec. Gtr. 4

Riff C1 - - - - - - - - - - - - - - - - - - -

mp

Elec. Gtr. 5 *(w/dist.)*

Riff C - - - - - - - - - - - - - - - - -

mf

You know, I tell her she's a nice piece of ass, ___ then her dad-dy punch-es me in the face. ___

So if you're pissed like ___ me, ___

Hate My Life - 8 - 6

_74_

bitch - es, here's what you got - ta do. _____

_76_ **G5**

Mm, put your mid - dle fing - ers up in the air, ___ go on ___ and say "F*** ___ you!" ___

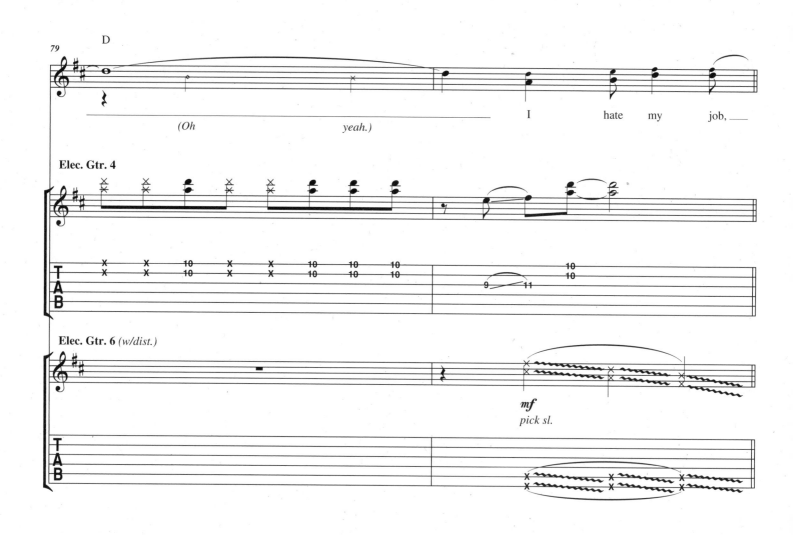

D

_79_

_____ I hate my job, ___

(Oh   yeah.)

Elec. Gtr. 4

Elec. Gtr. 6 _(w/dist.)_

_mf_
pick sl.

Chorus: (2:36)
w/Rhy. Fig. 1 _(Elec. Gtrs. 1-3 & 6, Acous. Gtr.)_
w/Riff A _(Elec. Gtr. 4)_   **w/Riff B** _(Elec. Gtr. 4) 13 times_

_81_ **A**

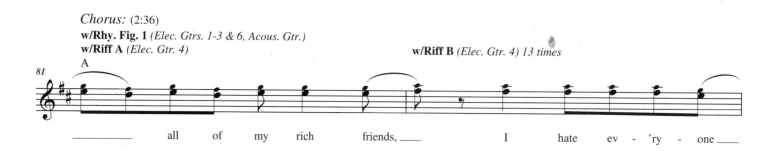

_____ all of my rich friends, ___ I hate ev - 'ry - one ___

_____ to the bit - ter end. _____ Noth - in' turns out right, _____ there's no _____ end in sight. _____

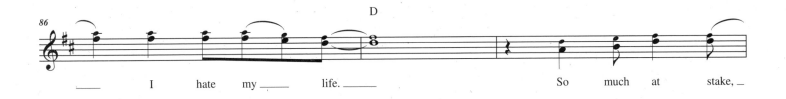

_____ I hate my _____ life. _____ So much at stake, _____

w/Rhy. Fig. 3 _(Elec. Gtrs. 1-3 & 6, Acous. Gtr.) meas. 5-8_

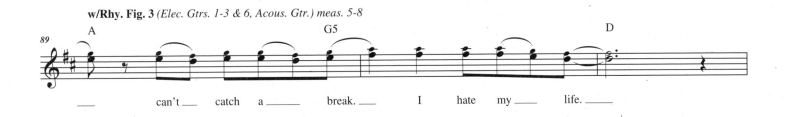

_____ can't _____ catch a _____ break. _____ I hate my _____ life. _____

w/Rhy. Fig. 3 _(Elec. Gtrs. 1-3 & 6, Acous. Gtr.) meas. 5-6_

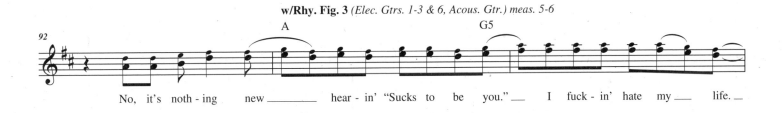

No, it's noth - ing new _____ hear - in' "Sucks to be you." _____ I fuck - in' hate my _____ life. _____

Elec. Gtrs. 1-3 & 6, Acous. Gtr.

_F***!_

Elec. Gtr. 4

Hate My Life - 8 - 8

HERO

*All gtrs. in Drop D, down 1/2 step:
⑥ = D♭ ③ = G♭
⑤ = A♭ ②= B♭
④= D♭ ①= E♭

Words and Music by
JOHN COOPER and KOREY COOPER

Moderately fast ♩ = 138 (w/half-time feel)

Intro:
N.C.

*Recording sounds a half step lower than written.

© 2009 WARNER-TAMERLANE PUBLISHING CORP., PHOTON MUSIC, LANDRUM PUBLISHING
and KOREY COOPER PUBLISHING DESIGNEE
All Rights on behalf of itself, PHOTON MUSIC and LANDRUM PUBLISHING
Administered by WARNER-TAMERLANE PUBLISHING CORP.
All Rights Reserved

Hero - 8 - 1

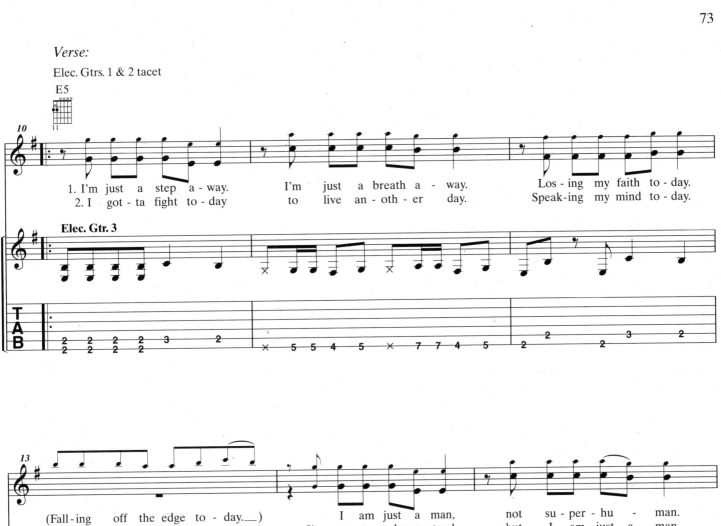

*Cue-size notes 2nd time only.

Hero - 8 - 2

74

Chorus:

LAST OF THE AMERICAN GIRLS

Lyrics by BILLIE JOE
Music by GREEN DAY

*Chords are implied.

3. She plays her

Guitar Solo:

MONSTER

*All gtrs. in Drop D, down 1 whole step:
⑥ = C   ③ = F
⑤ = G   ② = A
④ = C   ① = D

Words and Music by
JOHN COOPER and GAVIN BROWN

Moderately fast ♩ = 132

*Recording sounds a whole step lower than written.
**Elec. Gtr. 1 dbld. 2nd time.

The se-cret side of me, I nev-er let you see. I keep it caged_ but I can't con - trol it.

So stay a-way from me, the beast is ug - ly, I feel the rage_ and I just can't hold it.

2. It's scratch-ing on the walls, in the clos - et, in the halls. It comes a - wake_ and I
3. My se - cret side I keep hid un - der lock and key. I keep it caged_ but I

can't con - trol it. Hid-ing un - der the bed, in my bod - y, in my head. }
can't con - trol it. 'Cause, if I let him out, he'll tear me up, break me down. }

NEVER GONNA BE ALONE

Moderately slow ♩ = 68

Verses 1 & 2:

Words and Music by
CHAD KROEGER and MUTT LANGE

Never Gonna Be Alone - 6 - 1

NOTHING BUT THE WHOLE WIDE WORLD

*Gtr. in Drop D, with capo at 2nd fret:

⑥ = D ③ = G
⑤ = A ② = B
④ = D ① = E

Words and Music by
JAKOB DYLAN

Moderately slow ♩ = 72

Intro:

D5

Acous. Gtr. 1
Rhy. Fill 1 _____

Play 4 times

fingerstyle; hold throughout

*Recording sounds a whole step higher than written.

𝄋 *Chorus:*

D5

Rhy. Fig. 1

1. Noth-ing but the whole   wide world to gain._____   Noth-ing,__   noth-ing.__   Got
2. Noth-ing but the whole   wide world to gain._____   Noth-ing,__   noth-ing.__   Got
3. Noth-ing but the whole   wide world for us._____   Noth-ing,__   noth-ing.__   Wants
4. Noth-ing but the whole   wide world for one._____   Noth-ing,__   noth-ing.__   Give

*No background vocals on Chorus 1.

Nothing but the Whole Wide World - 4 - 1

Nothing but the Whole Wide World - 4 - 2

RAIN

All gtrs. in Open B5 tuning:
⑥ = B ③ = F♯
⑤ = F♯ ② = B
④ = B ① = B

Words and Music by
SCOTT STAPP and MARK TREMONTI

Moderately ♩ = 100

Intro:

Verse:

1. Can you help me out,___ can you lend___ me a hand?___ It's safe to say___ that I'm
2. I tried to fig-ure out,___ I can't un-der-stand___ what it means___ to be

stuck a-gain.___
whole a-gain.___
Trapped be-tween this life___ and the light,___ I just can't
Trapped be-tween the truth___ and the con-se-quence,___

___ fig-ure out,___
___ noth-ing's real,___
how to make it right.
no-thing's mak-ing sense.___

A

Rain - 7 - 2

Bridge:

Acous. Gtr. cont. simile

Elec. Gtr. 2 *(w/light dist.)*

mf

Elec. Gtr. 1

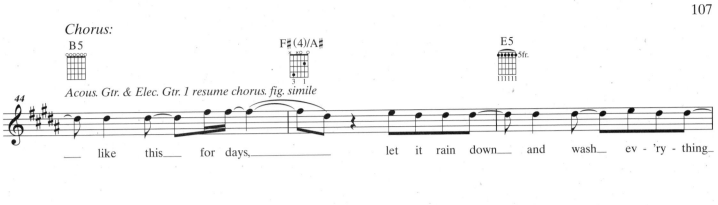

Chorus:

Acous. Gtr. & Elec. Gtr. 1 resume chorus. fig. simile

___ like this___ for days,_____ let it rain down___ and wash___ ev - 'ry - thing___

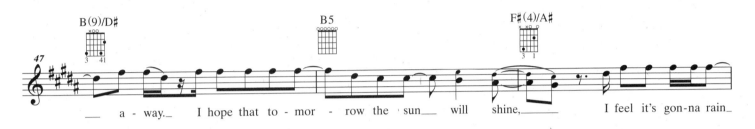

___ a - way.___ I hope that to - mor - row the sun___ will shine,_____ I feel it's gon - na rain___

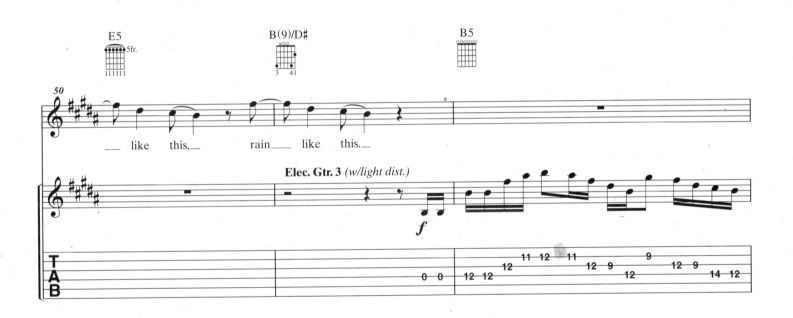

___ like this,___ rain___ like this.___

Elec. Gtr. 3 *(w/light dist.)*

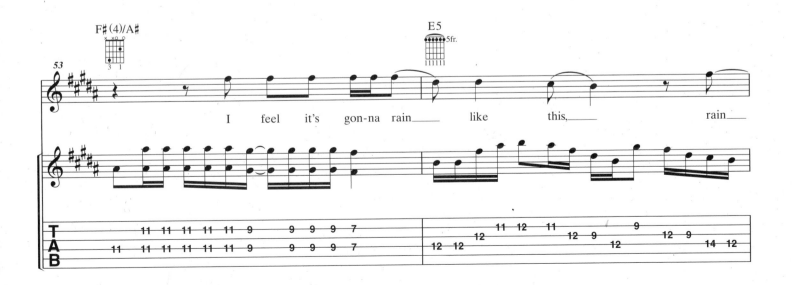

I feel it's gon - na rain____ like this,_____ rain____

RESISTANCE

Words and Music by
MATTHEW BELLAMY

$\mathigh = 135$

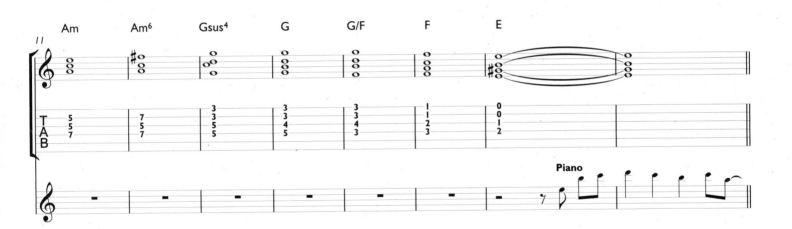

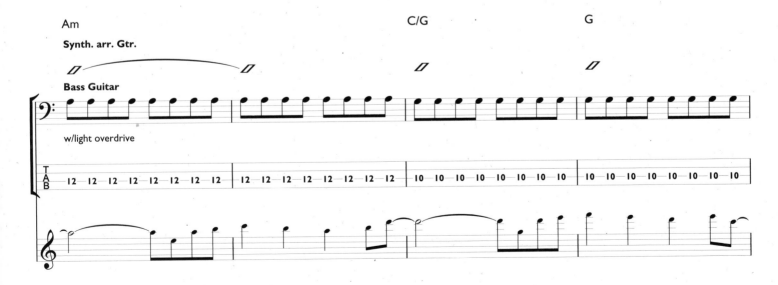

Resistance - 11 - 1

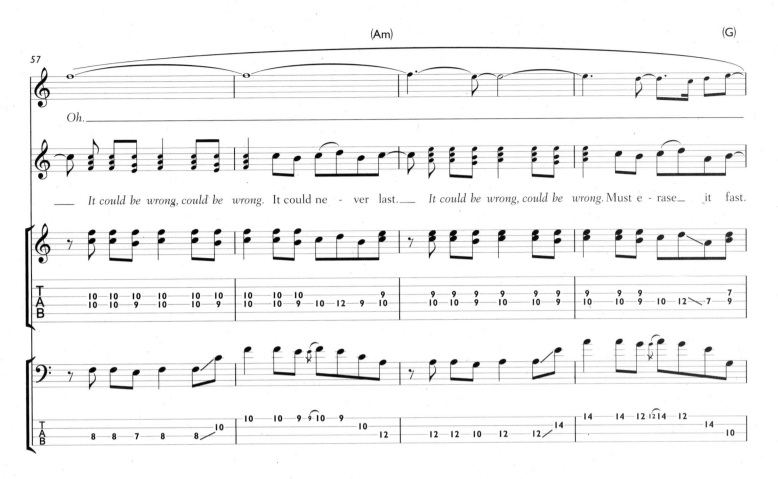

Oh.___

It could be wrong, could be wrong. It could ne - ver last.___ It could be wrong, could be wrong. Must e - rase___ it fast.

It could be wrong, could be wrong. But it could-'ve been right.___ It could be wrong, could be... This is our re -

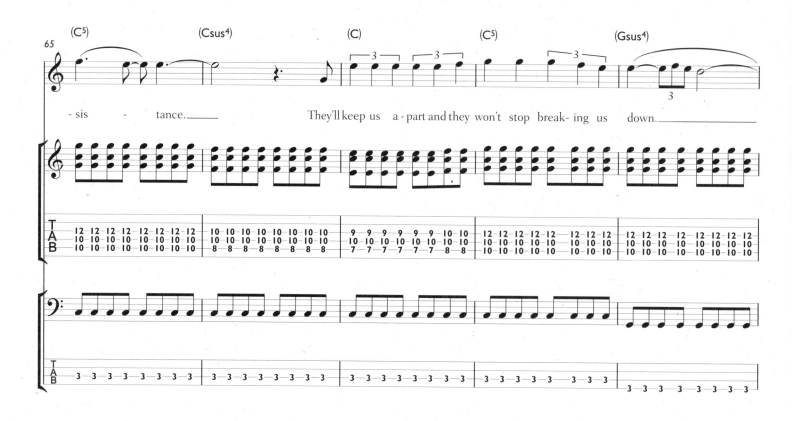

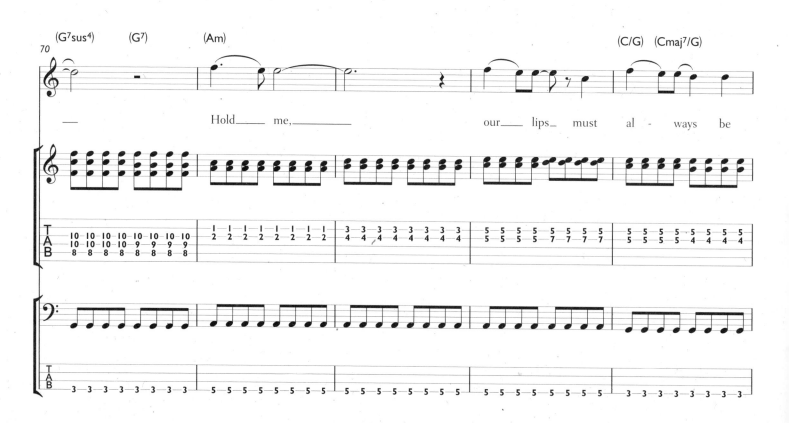

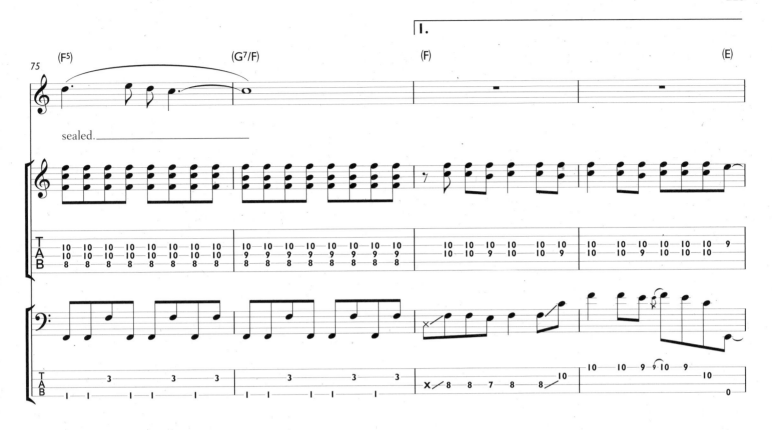

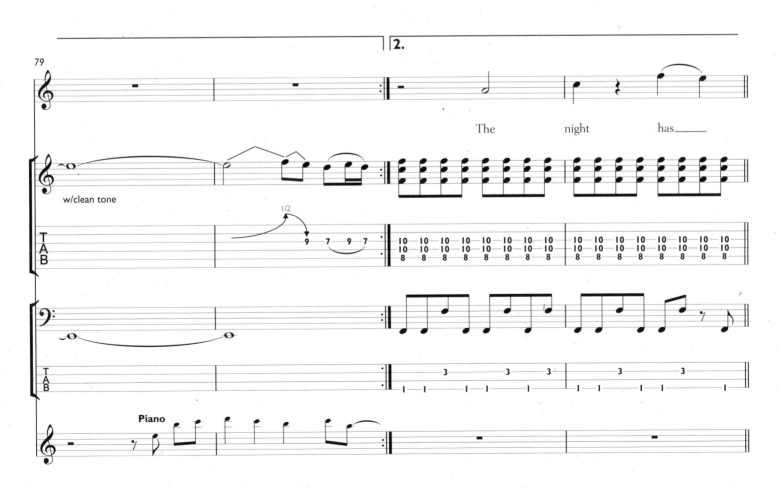

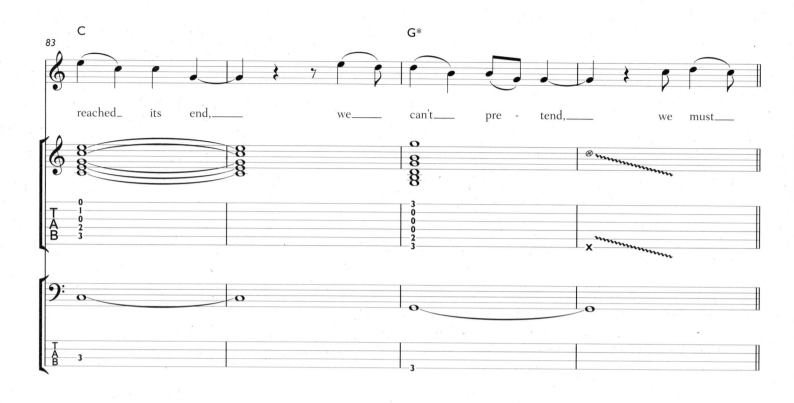

reached its end,_____ we_____ can't_____ pre - tend,_____ we must_____

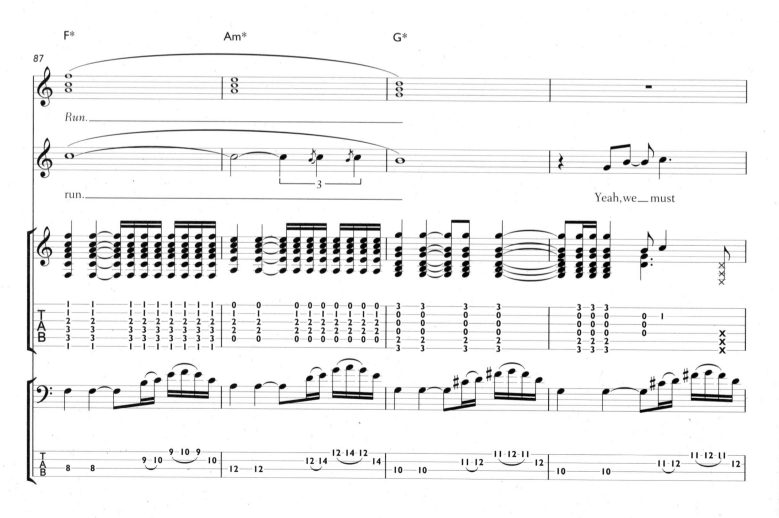

Run._____

run._____

Yeah, we_____ must

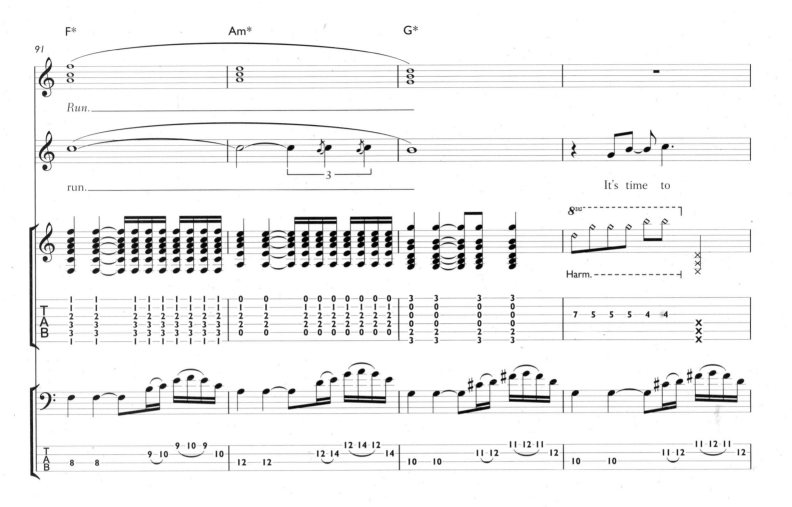

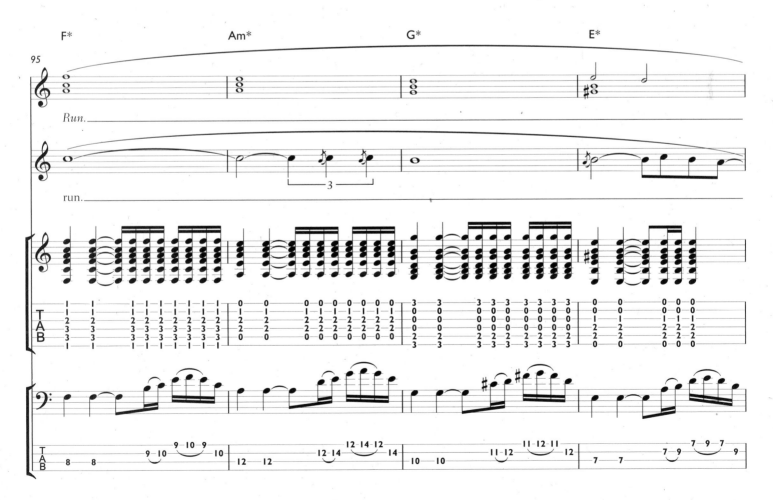

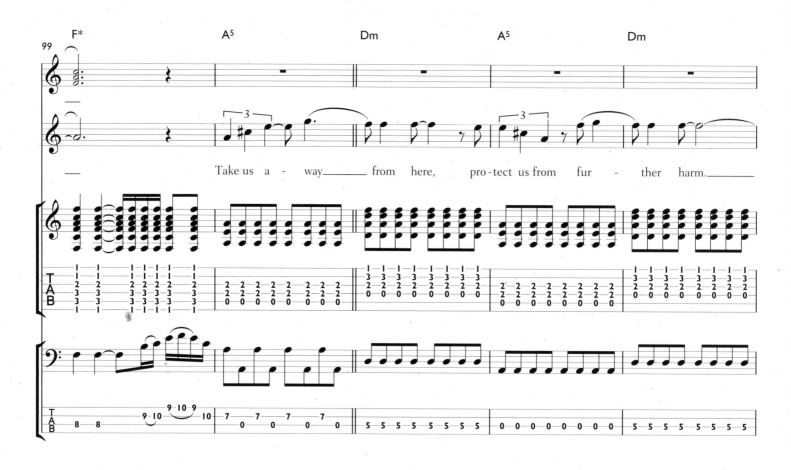

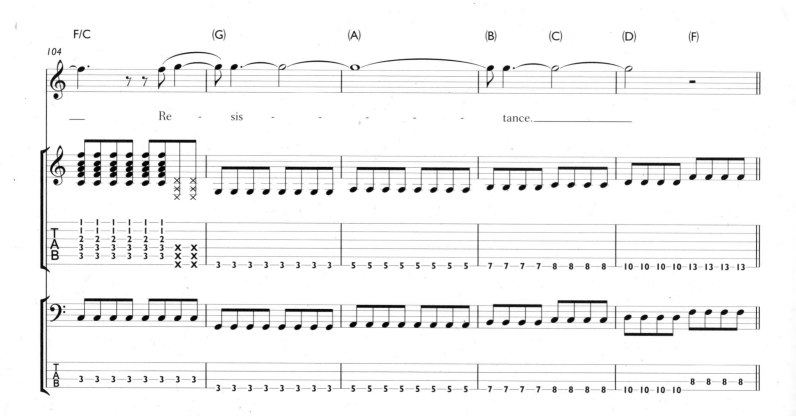

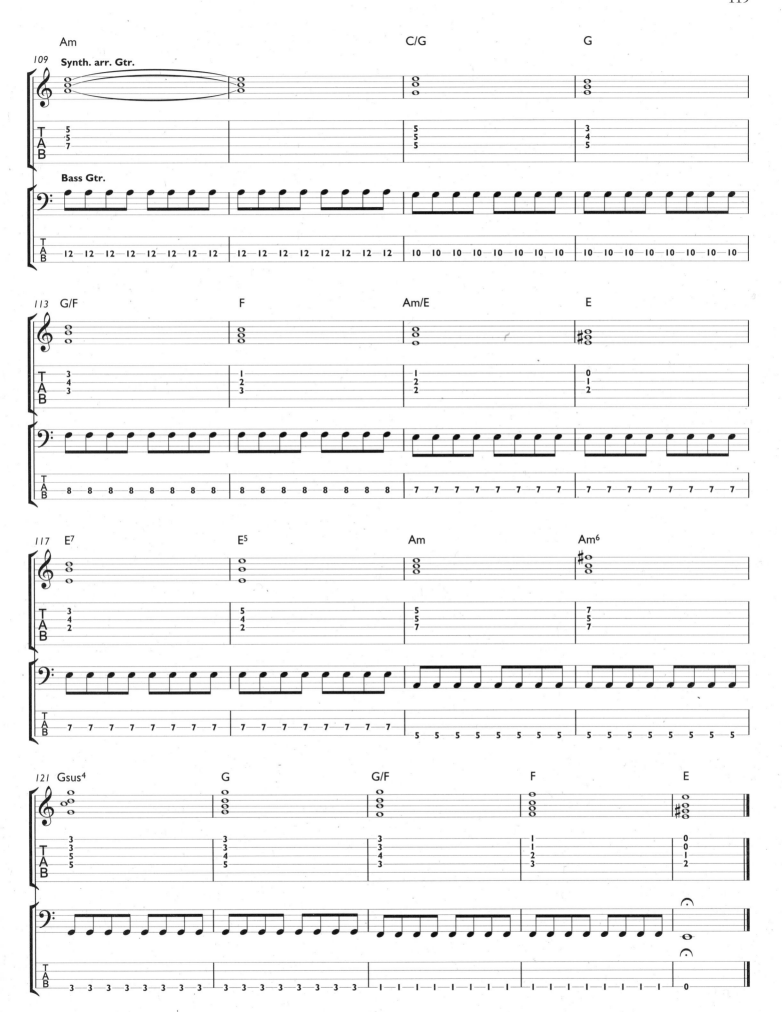

SHAKIN' HANDS

Words and Music by
CHAD KROEGER, JOEY MOI
and MUTT LANGE

All gtrs. in Drop D, ⑥ = D

Moderately slow ♩ = 76

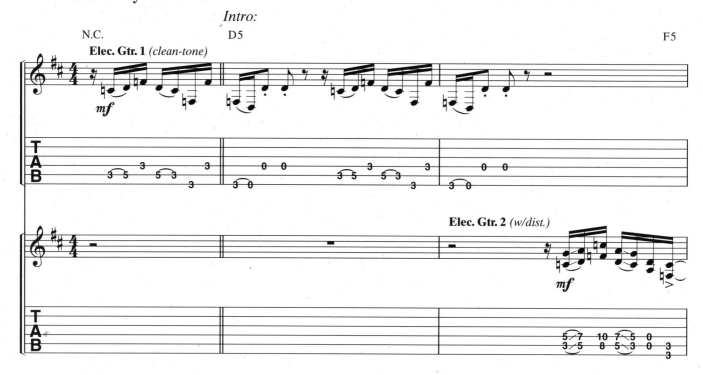

Verses 1 & 2:

eyes on the prize___ as the girl next door. You
(2.)e - ven let the dev - il buy her lit - tle black book. Cit - y

Rhy. Fig. 1A
Elec. Gtr. 3 *(clean-tone)*

Rhy. Fig. 1
Elec. Gtr. 1

grow up quick when you grow up poor.___ It's the
Hall would prob - 'bly fall if an - y - one got a look.___ Ev - 'ry

w/Rhy. Figs. 1 *(Elec. Gtr. 1)* **& 1A** *(Elec. Gtr. 3), both 4 times*

on - ly way to L. A. that she knows, the
"A list" play - er is a fa - vor - ite friend, says they

Shakin' Hands - 11 - 2

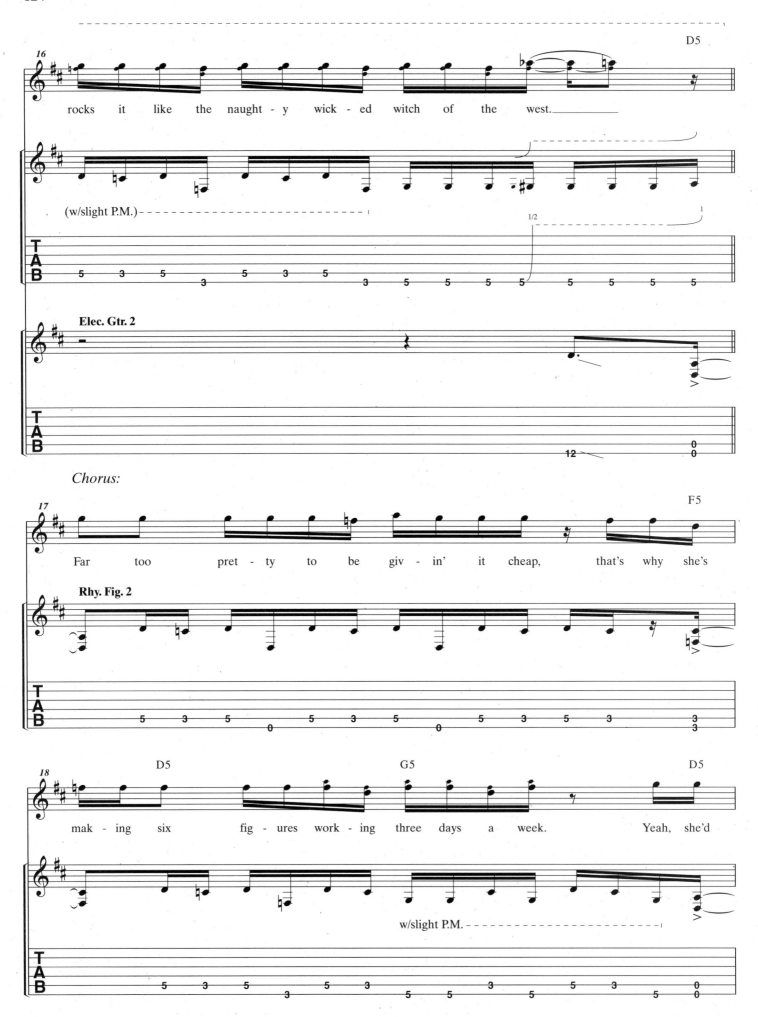

Chorus:

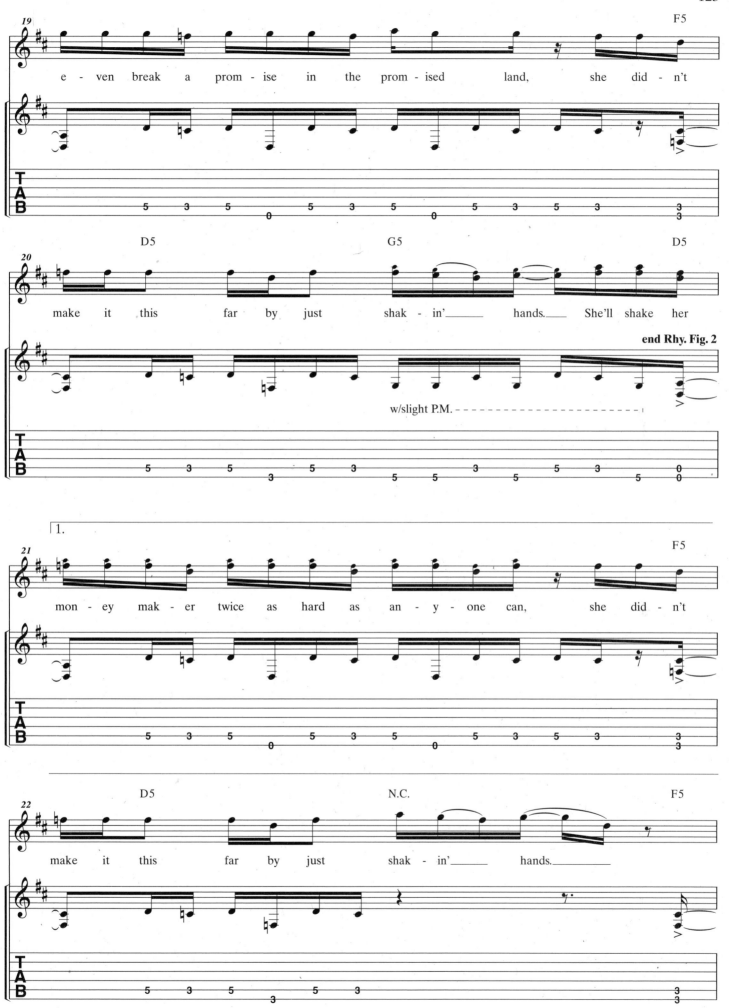

Verse 3:

Band tacet

some - one spilled the beans and now her name's in the press, tough to

keep it all a se - cret when you're one of the best.____ The

Chorus:

130

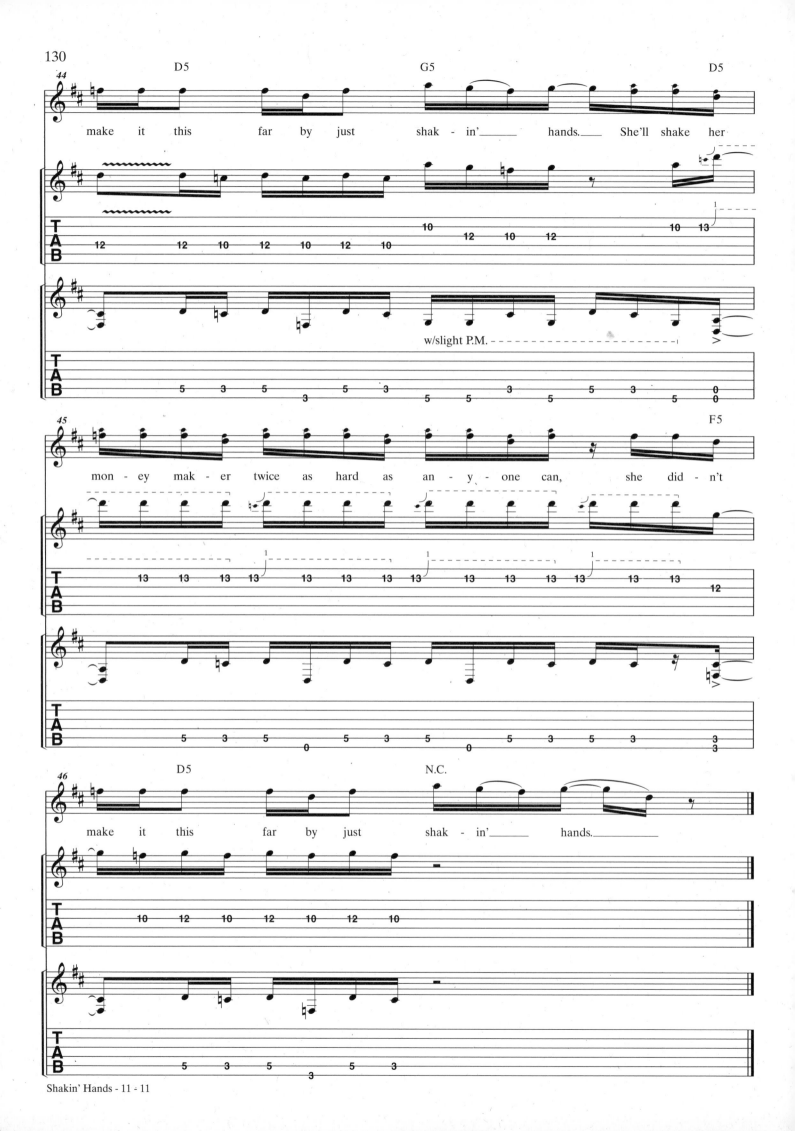

UPRISING

Words and Music by
MATTHEW BELLAMY

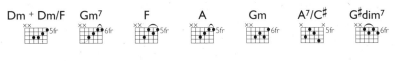

♩ = 127 **Swung**

Electric Guitar in drop-D tuning

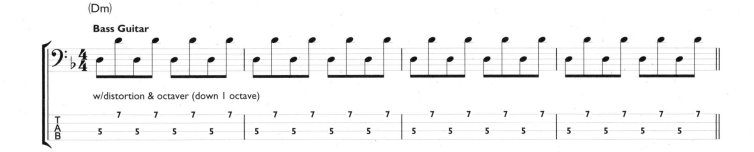

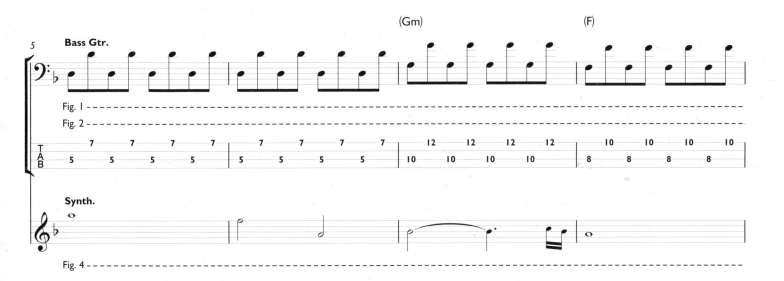

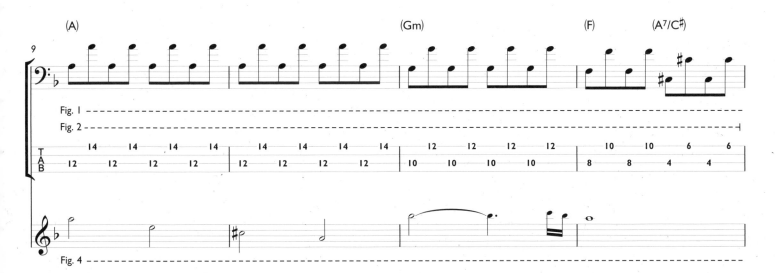

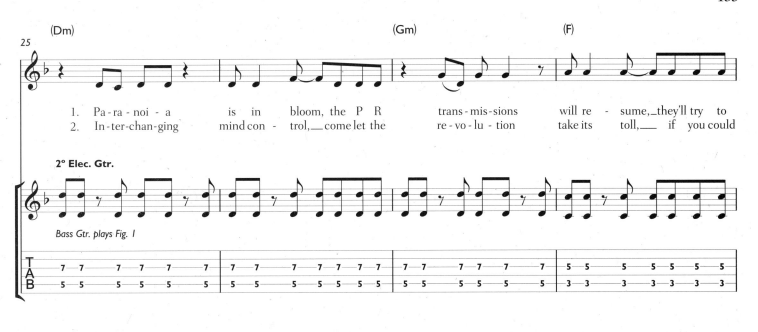

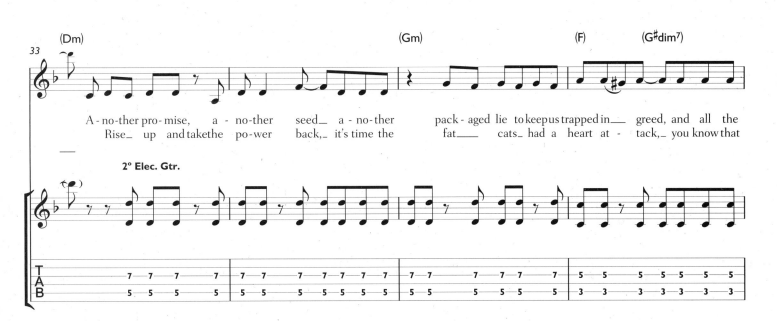

green belts wrapped a - round our_ minds, and end-less red tape to keep the truth con - fined.
their_time's co - ming to an_ end,_ we have to u - ni - fy and watch our flag as - cend.

(So come on.)

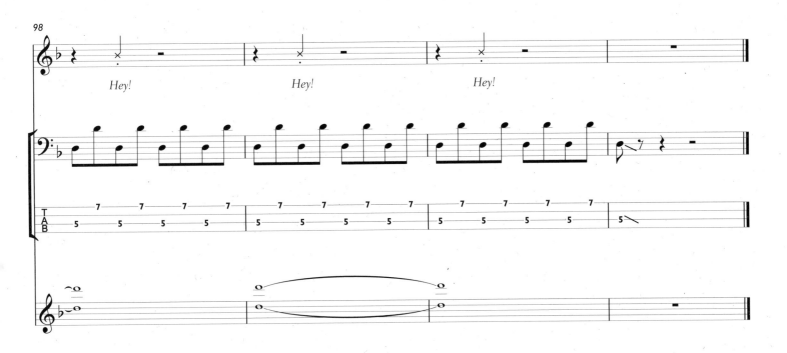

A THOUSAND FACES

*All gtrs. in Drop D, down 1 1/2 steps:
⑥ = B ③ = E
⑤ = F♯ ② = G♯
④ = B ① = C♯

Words and Music by
SCOTT STAPP and MARK TREMONTI

Moderately slow ♩ = 78

Intro:

*Recording sounds one and one half steps lower than written.

Verse:

Chorus:

Interlude:

you got-ta let it out,___ just let it out,___ you got-ta let it out.___

Chorus:

Lyrics:
You wear a thou- sand fac- es,

tell__ me which__ is you.__

Tell me which is

P.H.

Elec. Gtr. 2

WAKING UP IN VEGAS

Moderately ♩ = 126

Verse 1:

Words and Music by
KATY PERRY, ANDRESAS CARLSSON
and DESMOND CHILD

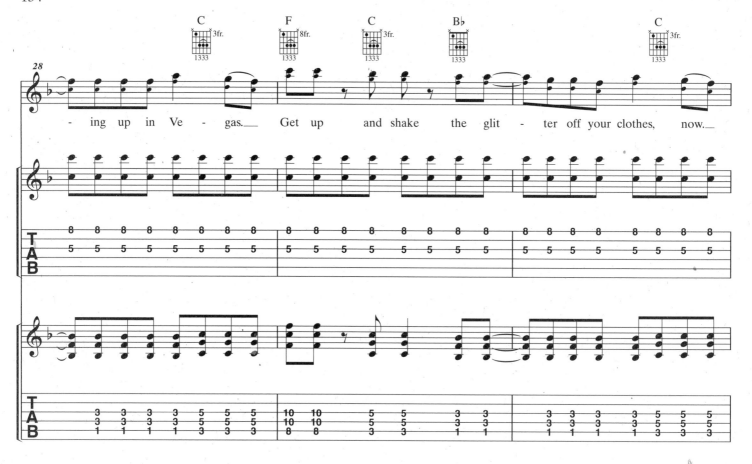

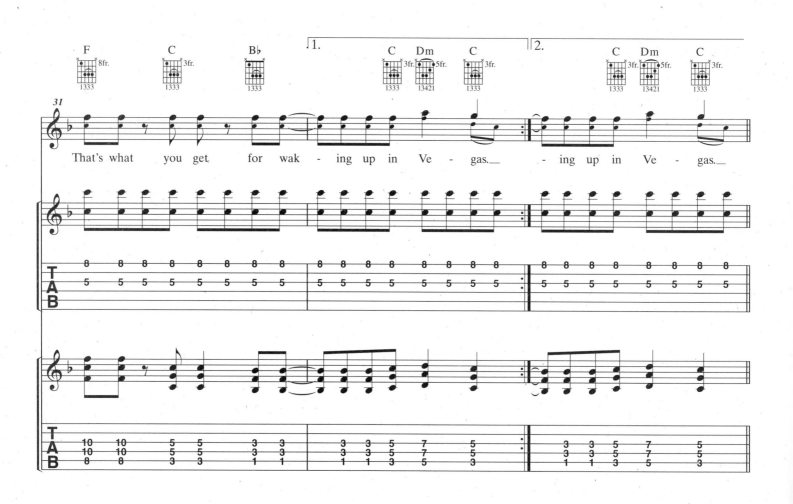

Pre-chorus:

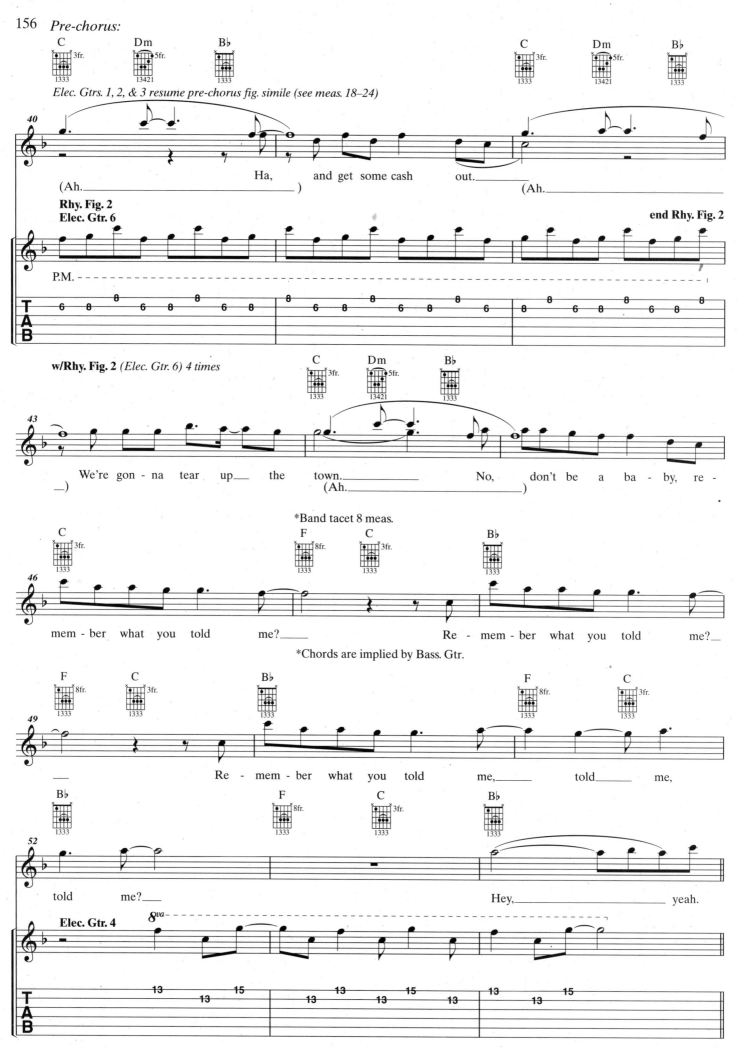

Chorus:

TABLATURE EXPLANATION

TAB illustrates the six strings of the guitar.
Notes and chords are indicated by the placement of fret numbers on each string.

String ⑥, 3rd fret   *String ①, 12th fret*   *A "C" chord*   *C chord arpeggiated*
String ③, 13th fret

BENDING NOTES

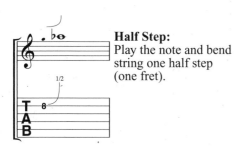

Half Step:
Play the note and bend
string one half step
(one fret).

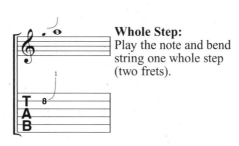

Whole Step:
Play the note and bend
string one whole step
(two frets).

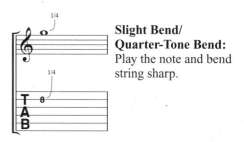

**Slight Bend/
Quarter-Tone Bend:**
Play the note and bend
string sharp.

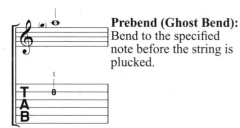

Prebend (Ghost Bend):
Bend to the specified
note before the string is
plucked.

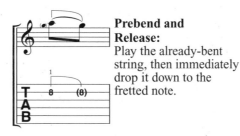

**Prebend and
Release:**
Play the already-bent
string, then immediately
drop it down to the
fretted note.

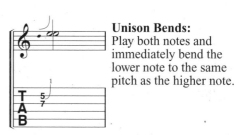

Unison Bends:
Play both notes and
immediately bend the
lower note to the same
pitch as the higher note.

**Bend and
Release:**
Play the note
and bend to
the next pitch,
then release
to the original
note. Only the
first note is
attacked.

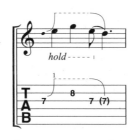

**Bends Involving
More Than One
String:**
Play the note and
bend the string
while playing an
additional note
on another string.
Upon release, re-
lieve the pressure from the additional note
allowing the original note to sound alone.

**Bends Involving
Stationary Notes:**
Play both notes and
immediately bend the
lower note up to pitch.
Return as indicated.

ARTICULATIONS

Hammer On:
Play the lower note, then "hammer" your finger to the higher note. Only the first note is plucked.

Pull Off:
Play the higher note with your first finger already in position on the lower note. Pull your finger off the first note with a strong downward motion that plucks the string—sounding the lower note.

Legato Slide:
Play the first note and, keeping pressure applied on the string, slide up to the second note. The diagonal line shows that it is a slide and not a hammer-on or a pull-off.

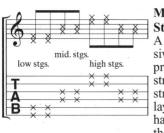

Muted Strings:
A percussive sound is produced by striking the strings while laying the fret hand across them.

Palm Mute:
The notes are muted (muffled) by placing the palm of the pick hand lightly on the strings, just in front of the bridge.

HARMONICS

Natural Harmonic:
A finger of the fret hand lightly touches the string at the note indicated in the TAB and is plucked by the pick producing a bell-like sound called a harmonic.

RHYTHM SLASHES

Strum Marks/ Rhythm Slashes:
Strum with the indicated rhythm pattern. Strum marks can be located above the staff or within the staff.

Single Notes with Rhythm Slashes:
Sometimes single notes are incorporated into a strum pattern. The circled number below is the string and the fret number is above.

Artificial Harmonic:
Fret the note at the first TAB number, lightly touch the string at the fret indicated in parens (usually 12 frets higher than the fretted note), then pluck the string with an available finger or your pick.

TREMOLO BAR

Specified Interval:
The pitch of a note or chord is lowered to the specified interval and then return as indicated. The action of the tremolo bar is graphically represented by the peaks and valleys of the diagram.

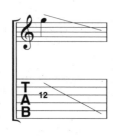

Unspecified Interval:
The pitch of a note or chord is lowered, usually very dramatically, until the pitch of the string becomes indeterminate.

PICK DIRECTION

Downstrokes and Upstrokes:
The downstroke is indicated with this symbol (⊓) and the upstroke is indicated with this (∨).